YOUR BEST LIFE

YOUR BEST LIFE

Pathways to Happiness

JUDITH COCHÉ, PH.D.

TABLE OF CONTENTS

TABLE OF CONTENTS

TABLE OF CONTENTS

For sixty families monthly for 35 years....
Thank you for teaching us
how to help you live your best lives

FOREWORD

How much do you want to live your best life day after day, decade after decade? Yes, it is easy to thrive when the universe provides easy choices. And no, life does not always cooperate: health falters, pets die, careers take dives, storms damage our best lives.

Positive Psychology has packaged age old wisdom to provide us with winning ways to approach life. The concepts mirror my own professional judgments, gleaned in 35 years of study and clinical practice in human development and existential psychology. Finally, we have guidelines to help each of us weather, and become stronger from, catastrophe, illness, aging and loss. Good stuff, this.

My own life acts as example of the need for a positive life stance. Without warning, my first husband died of a suddenly discovered metastatic melanoma at age 49. This brilliant and handsome man was also my career partner, leaving me to run The Coche Center and parent my daughter single handedly. I found myself emotionally stranded, needing to cover all bases on two home, and two practice locations filled with clients. Left a widow and single parent of a gifted, blossoming teen-age girl, I choose to apply my knowledge of optimal living to push through

1

cataclysmic disaster. This tragedy taught me foundation skills for my future.

These personal lessons, borne out of the grit that comes from necessity, inform the thinking behind the stories in this book. Using vignettes from my practice and my life, I published my newspaper column for The Cape May County Herald. I fictionalized names for privacy but kept the dynamics intact because stories teach us through example.

I began The Coche Center, LLC as a tiny practice in Clinical Psychology in 1978. We had no capital, no loans, and no clients. Insurance reimbursements did not exist for psychologists so survival was highly unlikely. Clients often felt ashamed of "needing" therapy. And yet we thrived. I think it is because feeling understood is necessary for all of us. Therapy provides us access to what is going on inside and allows us to make the unconscious our friend. It tames the wildness of loving another.

Each 800 word story started as a newspaper column between 2007 and today. Each is a metaphor for life. In the dedication of a cat owner who gives his water shy pet hydrotherapy, for example, we remember how powerful positive relationships are in our lives. My hope is that the stories take residence in your heart .

2013 marks the 35th anniversary of The Coche Center, LLC. As our 35th anniversary gift you, I hope these little stories contribute to the quiet sparkle of living your best life.

Judith Coche, Ph.D., A.B.P.P.
June 2013
Rittenhouse Square and Stone Harbor

INTRODUCTION

"Skill makes love unending."

• *Ovid*

I began writing a column for the residents of Cape May County in 2007 at the suggestion of Joe Zelnick, a beloved journalist who died too soon. The goal was to educate the residents of Cape May County about issues in mental health so that they could live their best lives. To keep it simple, I call the column, "Making Life Work."

Beginning a column felt a little like standing at the top of a mountain and singing a little melody into the wilderness. I was able to voice anything at all, but had no clue whether anybody was paying attention. At first the folks who told me how much they loved my column were personal friends, so I was not convinced of a readership. But copy editor Joan Nash supported my efforts, so I kept writing. In the second year, there was a noticeable stir among a forming readership. I would go to dinner at a local club, be introduced to someone I had never met, and hear

3

"Oh! Aren't you the person who writes the column, you're a... you're a.... are you a psychologist?"

Now, six years later, I know folks read "Making Life Work." Not long ago, a stranger called to ask for an appointment with me. When I asked whether she wanted to know something about me, she said "Not if you write your own columns. Do you?". When I said I did, she replied, "Then I know you are the right person for me to work with. I really like your columns because you help me to go deeper inside myself and leave me feeling better than I did before I read your column."

2013 marks the 35th anniversary of The Coche Center, LLC, a Practice in Clinical Psychology that specializes in helping individuals, couples and families maximize their lives. To mark this special event, it seemed fitting to honor our clients by sharing some of their stories, which have been fictionalized before publishing them in my column. Each column in this book highlights an aspect of optimal living. My goal is to make it very easy for the readier to grasp complex ideas, and remember them days later. 800 words can be ingested over half a bagel. The trick is to create a thread of meaning that leaves you, the reader, with something to consider for the rest of the day. I've always believed that plain language is the most powerful form of communication : saying something simply is more challenging than cloaking it in academic rhetoric. The columns speak simply.

People seek professional help with their life because they get stuck in a life issue and need to feel happier. In each column I address one of the five key concepts in creating PERMAnent wellbeing. I borrowed this list from Dr Martin Seligman and our mutual students of Positive Psychology at the University of Pennsylvania Medical School and Graduate Psychology departments, where I teach Psychiatric Residents and Psychology Graduate Students. As you read, I lead you into the uplifting world of positive emotions, engagement, positive relationships, meaning and accomplishment. In the twenty or so columns ahead, you catch a glimpse of how folks use their own internal and interpersonal tools to make life sing for them despite the tricky challenges they face.

Clients have struggled in my office since 1978 to wrap their brains and hearts around ways to change in desired directions. While changing, they have said amazing things about their own growth. In the final pages of the book, I share with you a few of the one liners from our clients about their own growth.

I hope that you find moments of pleasure and meaning in these brief essays. I hope they enable you to capitalize on the strength inside of you, so that you too may live your best life.

YOU ARE THE AUTHOR OF YOUR LIFE

"Whom shall I send?
And who will go for us?
And I said, here I am.
Send me."

- *Isaah 6:8 p 181*

Perfectly decked out in a navy suit that complemented his gray-ing temples and steel blue eyes, Brad chose his words carefully. "We earn plenty of money as financial advisors but we work too long and hard. We have a summer home we rarely get to. We de-serve to be happier. I want us to live on less money and retire by 55 so that we can enjoy our lives together. Who knows how long we will live? Let's cut back. We deserve to flourish in our lives."

Ann, tall, lithe and elegant, listened. Each time Brad brought up this theme she reminded him that she had grown up in fi-nancial need, and she loved her work. But ever since Brad had read the psychological research that tells us that money is not highly related to happiness, Brad had become tenacious about creating an optimal life without wealth. Accomplished at sales presentations, he made an impressive pitch. As the three of us sat together week after week, he did influence her towards shifting her primary motivation from material comfort to well being.

Curiosity engaged, Ann wanted to understand the major concepts behind Brad's aspirations, but she worried that he might spin the facts to be more convincing. Because she trusted my knowledge of the field, she turned to me. "Judith, I want to know more about the ingredients that go into being satisfied with life. Is there a list or something? Do we even know?"

"Ann, I can highlight the major ideas about what helps us to flourish in our lives. The list makes perfect sense. We surmise that there are five properties that go with feeling daily well-being. Each of these ways of being are so satisfying that we want to be involved in them simply because they feel good. I remember these activities through their first initials, which spell PERMA."

•Positive emotion: When we concentrate on creating pleasure, comfort and a warm feeling inside, we create the very cornerstone of experiencing well being. We stop planning and simply flow with the pleasant feeling state. Sometimes we even experience ecstasy. A bubbly Jacuzzi or dancing with someone you love might create this for you.

•Engagement: When we are fully engaged in something, time stops and we can lose ourselves in the activity. We do not bother to stop to reflect or to think. When Brad is running in a marathon, he is fully engaged.

•Relationships: We actually know that happiness is about being with other people. People you love are the best antidote to feeling badly. And doing kind acts, like bringing flowers to a sick friend, usually creates a short burst of well-being.

• Meaning: We need meaning in our lives. We need to work towards something we believe in. "Brad places great meaning in molding a best life for you and for him. Ann, you find meaning in helping others make money. For most of us, building such strong relationships provides optimal meaning."

• Accomplishment: It feels good to set and achieve a goal. Some of us want to earn enough money to later donate to worthy causes. Others of us get a sense of achievement from collecting sea glass or running a marathon. The joy is actually in exerting mastery over our environment. We achieve because it feels great to achieve.

These five characteristics of people who flourish give us clues about how to have a terrific life day after day. Folks who flourish are optimistic, self-reliant, resilient to stress, and successful in creating vibrant human relationships.

But the best news of all is that we can train people to flourish. We think of this as psychological fitness, whether this fitness be related to emotional fitness, social resilience, spiritual depth, optimal physical health, or family vibrancy. As Gandhi said, we can actually become the embodiment of the change we want to see in the world. As pie-in-the-sky as this sounds, Gandhi's statement can function as a wonderful road map for optimal life.

A way that I think about this is that we are able to take ownership and to become the author of our lives. We can turn trauma into growth. We can become fully accountable. The Bible tells us that when God asked Isaiah whom to send into a dangerous situation requiring bravery, vision and leadership, Isaiah replied, "Here I am. Send me."

To consider: Am I on the road to flourishing in my life? How might my life improve if I trained myself to be more accountable and have more meaningful relationships with those I love?

POSITIVE EMOTIONS

I INTEND TO ENJOY IT

A fresh cancer diagnosis is pretty hard to stomach, especially if it enters a life filled with success and joy. Leslie is a petite brunette with big brown eyes and hair pulled into a pony tail under a "Stone Harbor" baseball cap much of the summer. Husband Josh and she engineer a steady stream of adult kids, grand kids and friends who vacation with them at their beach house. Thrilled with her life, Leslie happily loads a station wagon full of family to summer outings to the Zoo and the crabbing dock in nearby Avalon.

"I need to deal with this sudden cancer diagnosis, and my family is going crazy." Leslie caught my gaze and kept it. She was not afraid. "Sure it is awful. I need chemo and I will hate it. My Father died from this at 73. But it will do me no good to worry so I'll get the chemo and see where we go from there. Meanwhile we have summer in Stone Harbor, and plan to corral Josh so that we can have fun. I intend to enjoy it and to get Josh on board. Life is what happens before you die, and I intend for us to savor our time here. Do you see anything wrong with that?"

I smiled. Before I answered Leslie, my mind jumped back 20 years to my first marriage. My then husband, Dr. Erich Coche, had been stricken with metastatic melanoma at age 48. During the last summer before his untimely death at 49, we savored the long days in our Stone Harbor duplex, jumping off our dock into the fresh lagoon and sailing the 26" hobby that held his rapt attention. During what was to be his last summer, Erich and tiny daughter Juliette and I did all the usual things: we walked The Point and wave jumped at the Nun's beach. We made mincemeat of two pound lobsters on my Labor Day birthday, and biked to Wildwood for Greek dinners. When he died 6 short months later, Erich summarized, "I have loved my life. I would change nothing. I just wish it were longer."

My heart was filled with sadness at Leslie's complex future, just as it had been grief stricken at the crashing blow of a metastatic cancer death warrant for my best buddy and life partner. But I applauded her courage and her optimism. Optimism is easy when life offers pleasant alternatives, but Leslie had created a mind set of positive energy that equipped her to manage her cancer well.

"Wow. Your determination is impressive! It is a pity that you are more courageous and upbeat than your panicked family but they are lucky that you are. The very optimism that has created the success you enjoy in your life has followed you into this nasty illness. Optimism is a powerful soldier against cancer. Keep it up!"

Optimism is key in adult happiness and in building happy marriages. "Finding the good thing" does not mean overlooking the tragedy that visits all of us at some time. Instead, we seize on what life dishes out as a way to develop new parts of ourselves. Optimism allows us to find the good thing in a complex situation. We develop a way to look on the favorable side of life events, expect the most favorable outcome and hold fast to the belief that good ultimately predominates over evil in the world. And, to some extent, thinking actually does make it so.

The Optimism Scale (LOT-R) has been used widely in research. I have summarized it below. Answer honestly, then tally the number of optimistic responses. Answer according to your own feelings, rather than how you think. Give each question an A,B,C,D, or E, (A = I agree a lot; B = I agree a little; C = I neither agree nor disagree; D = I Disagree a little; E = I Disagree a lot) .

Then tally how optimistic your life attitude is. Are you pleased?

- In uncertain times, I usually expect the best.(A)
- If something can go wrong for me, it will.(E)
- I'm always optimistic about my future. (A)
- I hardly ever expect things to go my way.(E)
- I rarely count on good things happening to me.(E)
- Overall, I expect more good things to happen to me than bad.(A)

Optimists accept the inevitable lemons in our life, squeeze them hard, and wring out the lemonade hidden in the sour fruit. Whether or not we know about Mary Poppins, some of us seem to know that just a spoonful of sugar helps the medicine go down. I invite you to join that camp.

To consider: How can you "find the good" in life like the optimists you know? How would your life be sweeter and juicier if you did?

JUDITH COCHÉ, PH.D.

ADAPTABILITY IS MY MIDDLE NAME

Opening the door to my waiting room I found Tamara standing on crutches, streaked greying blond hair offset by deep brown eyes and a big smile. Next to her was husband Len, a small older man with piercing eyes and balding head, holding an empty wheel chair. Surprised by the greeting, I waited for an explanation.

"We got halfway here, but the bumpy sidewalk popped the wheel off. It was too hard to hobble the five blocks back home, so we kept walking to keep the appointment. "Tamara looked wiped out. I'll stay and Len will get me and the chair in an hour."

"How is the aftermath of the accident?" Tamara had smashed her ankle pedaling down a steep Hawaiian mountain, and had been flown in to Penn. Surgery successful, she was trying to maneuver the sudden changes required in a complex life.

"I can't get into my tiny office with my leg and the wheelchair, so I am working from home but I need administrative support." A highly respected accountant, Tamara's clients need her assistance year round. "It is weird to have a full time nurse giving me a shower but I pretend I am at a spa so I somehow make that work. Len finds me hard to live with these days because I am so devoid of things to do that I chatter and nibble incessantly. But all in all we are coping just like we always have."

Tamara and Len sought help for a comfortable 38 year marriage that needed an infusion of passion and fun. Part of the "fix" was an exotic vacation, different from their customary weekend in museum-filled London. The biking adventure was a stretch for them: Len had been worried about safety, but Tamara cajoled him into going by extolling the virtues of new activities. "I have to give Len credit: he has not even insinuated that this is my own d--- fault, though I bet he thinks just that."

"How have you adapted to this", I asked, knowing she depended on her considerable income to support Len's unexpected retirement from corporate executive status.

"Adaptability is my middle name. You know that. I can't afford to let details get me down. I'd never be where I am if Len and I hadn't bounced with a ton of punches." I recalled aloud that they had rebuilt their center city town home after a surprise fire spread the smell of smoke throughout the 120 year old building. And how they had helped their rebellious adolescent daughter cope with scoliosis. And I commended Tamara again for her creativity in handling Len's prostate cancer, which left impairment in their love life. Tamara had good naturedly learned a special technique which enabled them to spice up this lifelong marriage despite his illness. "It is a nuisance but he is so relieved to feel normal that it is worth it. "

"Tamara, do you know that adaptability is one of the key factors in people who show resilience and strength during their lives?" I wanted her to hear well-deserved acknowledgement of their coping skills. "You and Len have clearly achieved your place of honor in the adaptability Hall of Fame."

"Thanks." She smiled. "It is actually fun for me to figure out things that seem to stump other people. I just don't know why they let this stuff get them down."

I caught her eye, and smiled. "Your adaptive problem solving has insured you optimal life resilience. You deserve the fruits of your labors." And I meant it.

Resilience is one of the secrets to optimal life development. Tamara illustrates what we, at The Coche Center, refer to as The Adaptability Tool Box. Some individuals and couples have personalities with a built-in, at-the-ready tool box to adapt to what life inevitably dishes out. The Adaptability Tool Box includes motivation, humor, cognitive flexibility and creativity. When things do not go well, some people use their imagination and courage to do something different, creating a solution where none existed. They manage to laugh at what life brings rather than giving in, finding humor and strength especially during hardship. They are actually proud of their ability to outwit challenges. This confidence about their own capacity allows them to muster creativity where others give up. Their resilience and problem solving ability is one of their greatest gifts.

To consider: In recent months, what has stumped you in your life? Might there be a more adaptable way to handle this? How might that be an advantage?

LEMONS TO LEMONADE

Last week The Coche Center Clinical Team integrated recent advances in our understanding of resiliency, the ability to bounce back from the punches life provides. We found expertise from Drs. Reivich, Schatte and Wolin, and created five characteristics of resilient people:

1. Positive world view: The ability to find the good things in life and live with optimism and hope.

2. Relationship-centered : The ability to engage others with empathy and reciprocity, making fulfilling connections to other people; also called "secure attachment".

3. Applied intelligence: the ability to think independently and reflectively about self and life, distancing emotionally and physically from the sources of trouble in one's life and to reflect and learn from them.

4. Grit: The determination to succeed by tenaciously taking the initiative and using one's power to impact one's world.

5. Adaptability Tool Box: The ability to integrate motivation, humor, and creativity in living life. The ability to use imagination and to have courage to do something different, creating some-

19

thing where nothing was. The ability to find humor even in hardship.

Let's concentrate on the need to maintain a positive world view. Optimism, and the ability to find hope even in hardship, is a hallmark of those who enjoy success throughout their life. Being resilient involves hope about the future: a positive outlook allows us to muster creativity where others give up.

Lanna is a living example of this hopefulness. A petite 65-year-old grandmother, Lanna recently retired after a spectacular career as an antiques dealer. She traveled annually to France, importing the finest quality provincial furniture, then selling her treasures to high end decorators at a substantial profit. Despite the small likelihood of succeeding in international furniture sales, Lanna's infectiously impish personality charmed her customers: interior designers around the Eastern seaboard consulted Lanna for their most discriminating clients. Recently, as her desire to spend more time with her family increased, Lanna cut back her business, inviting her family to their ocean front home in Stone Harbor, where she gladly fed, housed and cared for three rambunctious grandsons.

I met with Lanna recently because of a worrisome recent medical diagnosis. She was told she has early stage melanoma, a skin cancer that can be deadly. Lanna reported that her husband, Jim, was beside himself with worry. "He is horrible to live with. He thinks of nothing else and has already begun thinking about updating my will. I have to tell you, I am not nearly as upset as everyone around me. Friends are looking worried when they greet me, and my kids are so hush-hush about this that I can't really even discuss it with them. The docs tell me that this is early stage and quite treatable. I have found the best care at Penn, and will do the needed medical stuff. I know this will be hard, but I love my life and I do not intend to get depressed. But I wish others could be upbeat with me. The people around me are more discouraging than the diagnosis! If everyone would just be a chipper as the docs, this would be much easier."

As I listened to Lanna work effectively with the diagnosis she had just been given, I realized that she possesses one of the greatest gifts in being human: she has the natural capacity and the psychological ability to turn lemons into lemonade. Like lemonade, her diagnosis remains bitter to the taste and she is not minimizing its danger. But, just as lemons offer their bitterness so that we humans can create nourishing dishes, Lanna automatically began to strategize how to turn her sour diagnosis into a workable plan that leads her back to a full life as soon as is humanly possible.

Is there any truth to the widely held belief that a positive outlook can even help us beat cancer?

Dr. Timothy Moynihan, M.D., cancer expert at the Mayo Clinic, reports that, while there is no scientific proof that a positive attitude improves the chance of a cure from cancer, a positive attitude can improve the quality of life during cancer treatment and beyond. Lanna's resiliency allows will allow her to be active and to maintain ties to friends which feeds her sense of well-being and provides her with needed strength to deal with the likely medical complexities in her future.

To consider: In the face of a terrifying diagnosis, which resiliency skills do I possess and how could I put them to good use? Would I?

JUDITH COCHÉ, PH.D.

SAILOR'S TIMELESS WISDOM

"An animal's eyes have the power to speak a great language"
• *Martin Buber*

At 108 human years, our grand dog, Sailor Anderson, has been in better physical shape. She is mostly blind, totally deaf, and constantly has to convince her hind legs that they still work. Last night we found her staring at a wall, looking lost. But in her 14 Portuguese water dog years of life, she has been an unfailing source of constant cheer. Blessed with a full body of silky white hair with irresistibly cute random patches of black, she is a delight to behold and pure pleasure to touch. Give her just the teensiest liver treat, and her tail still wags so hard that her back end shimmies.

For the last six summers, Sailor has visited us often at our cottage, which we refer to as "Sailor's summer camp." She knows exactly how to enjoy her vacation. She alternates between sunning herself on our deck, staring vacantly at the sparkling sunlit bay, and hanging out at the kitchen in hopes of dropped food morsels. On beach outings she heads straight for the ocean, snarfing up all the smelly beach treats she can grab on the way, then runs full tilt at water's edge. Wet, sandy and happy, she has to be dragged back to the car.

But Sailor is very old. Many owners would have "put her out of her misery," since her senses and mobility are so impaired. Cadi and Scott, our adult kids who own Sailor, have observed that she seems quite content to live each day with many joyful moments. And many of us humans could benefit from Sailor's take on life. She demonstrates the secret to happiness for us all.

For Sailor, each waking moment involves pleasure seeking. She seeks pats, sunny spots, food of all varieties, her "pack" of dogs and family, bowls of fresh water, a place to relieve herself, and soft bedding for deep and lengthy sleep. In her waking hours, she throws herself into a dedicated quest to acquire moment after moment of pleasure. Last night sautéing salmon lured her from the softly plump kidney-shaped bed she stole from our dog, Whitby, to the kitchen where I was cooking dinner. Planting herself stubbornly between my knees, she managed to shadow my moves as I went from counter to fridge to stove to ready dinner. Nose poised from the smell of the salmon, she then planted herself at our table, waiting her turn for fallen morsels and post-dinner pats, as though she were certain that cuddles and leftovers are the goal of a life well lived. And perhaps they are.

If Sailor could read the philosophy of positive existentialism or a review of happiness research, she would know how finely tuned her instincts are. Philosophers of meaning, like Martin Buber and Albert Camus, direct us to manage daily anxiety in order to carve out meaning and well being despite inevitable threats to our health and financial security. Whether you have two naked legs, or four fuzzy ones, whether physically fit or disabled, for many of us, moments of pure joy come from great food, blissful slumber, and the colors of sunset. In the equivalent of her 108th human year, Sailor models for us Camus' wisdom: "In the midst of winter, I finally learned that there was in me an invincible summer."

We now have research on what creates a sense of well being in humans. We know that the state of being called happiness comes to us each day if we create multiple moments of the feeling that life is good. The best news of all is that happiness does not depend on wealth or perfect health, but defies the disabilities created by old age and physical limitations. Well being is actually a state of mind reached through the courage to create multiple pockets of pleasure in each of our waking days.

Sailor, with a wag of your tail and your continued search for the perfect treat, thanks to you for inspiring us humans to face up to our own limitations. We have lots to learn from pups like you.

To consider: How can I create my life such that each day provides me with a minimum of 25 moments where I feel content and happy? Do I deserve this much happiness? What might I need to change in my life as I know it, in order to create happy days?

ENGAGEMENT

HOW CAN YOU CREATE HAPPINESS?

Baby goats. Fresh hay smell. Pansies. Marsh grass greening. Sunlight streaming. Biking. Convertibles. Naked-toed sandals. Spring makes many of us happy. But what is happiness anyway?

For much of my career as a clinical psychologist it has been unacceptable to try to help clients in therapy feel happier. I was trained to offer less: less depression, less anxiety, less smoking, less anger. Clinical Psychology was pathology-driven; goal was to feel less sick, not necessarily in top shape or to promote well being. We healed symptoms, like headaches and overeating, but we did not help create ideal lives. Around 1985, we began to understand that we do need to treat and prevent illness, but that we can help folks live optimal lives. Just as we have been brushing our teeth daily to prevent tooth decay, and paying dentists high fees when we slack off in our own prevention, we have begun to shout to all who will listen that we can help people be happier.

• We can prevent high percentages of divorce by teaching simple couples skills

27

• We can prevent future depression through behavioral treatment

• We can promote well being through coaching skills in how to think positively

Impressive indeed, but now that happiness has finally become an acceptable goal for all of us to achieve, what is happiness? Our Clinical Psychology intern Stephen Schueller, is as fascinated by happiness as I am, so we looked into what we know about happy individuals. How do we define happiness? What does it consist of?

Let's consider Byron's daily grind. Byron likes to work out, to have a nice car, and to laugh with his girlfriend. He is goal driven and ambitious. But his ulcers attack him daily, causing him unbearable pain and intense medical treatment. He refuses to do therapy because it is that "touchy feely stuff." Byron is never going to be able to achieve a substantial level of daily well being to qualify as feeling happy. Happiness is primarily a highly personal, subjective state that depends on how you feel and how you think. If I ask Byron whether he is happy, he looks thoughtful, pauses, then answers carefully "Sometimes. Yes. Sometimes I think I am, when my ulcers aren't acting up."

By refusing to do treatment for internal stress, Byron has overlooked his own power to influence his thoughts by making them more constructive. Byron can absolutely help his body to relax by learning to direct his thoughts and feelings into more positive channels. I promise you that he has the power to reduce his physical discomfort by training his thoughts and feelings. Byron can actually increase his own happiness.

If Byron entered treatment, he would quickly learn to practice cognitive self-discipline. I would teach him to direct his thoughts towards what I call the Lucky 7 qualities of a happy person. These lucky 7 are based on current thinking about increasing well-being and promoting happiness. To help you get your own happiness score, I have turned these qualities into seven True or False questions:

1. I tend to look on the bright side of things and am often thought of as an optimistic person by those who know me well.
2. I enjoy living in the here and now and making the most of every moment in life, especially my daily experiences.
3. I feel a deeper connection and commitment to a larger sense of meaning and purpose in my life, whether or not this involves a belief in a higher being.
4. For me, happiness is other people and the investment I make in the relationships I treasure.
5. I pursue my goals as a person and enjoy achieving goals I set.
6. I make time to help others and to donate my energies to enhancing the lives of other people, be they family or strangers.
7. I feel not only deserving of good things but grateful when I reap benefits of my life, whether or not I express this gratitude.

So, now that you know what we ask clients to see how happy they are, how did you fare? And how can you apply it to your life as an individual, whether singled or coupled?

To consider: How many questions did you honestly answer with a rousing "Yes?" What might you do to increase your "Yes" score? And how much might it benefit your life? If you take on this project to increase your own happiness, do let me know. I'll be rooting for you.

BIRTH ROW, FRONT AND CENTER

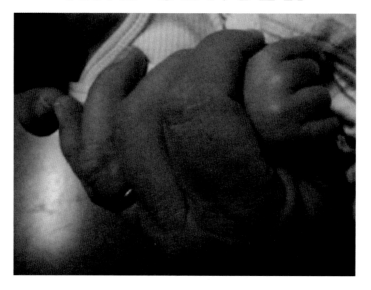

3:45 a.m.: "Mom, we are bringing Ava over…now." I could not be more wide-awake. I get to shepherd my three-year-old granddaughter while her Mom and Dad go to the birthing suite. Then, I join them to welcome their unborn daughter, who has decided to be born any minute.

4:30 a.m.: Forget getting the child to sleep. We do chocolate chip cookies and milk (two cookies). "Grammy, Sara is going to pop out…she is going to pop out Grammy…" Yup. Indeed.

5:15 a.m.: "Grammy, can we cuddle in your big bed?" Now? You bet. Good Night Moon and three songs later, Ava is sound asleep. I am not. I wait to be called to the birth of a person.

5:45 a.m.: "Juliette has asked that you come now." Michael, son-in-law extraordinaire, sounds calm. I know better. I high-tail it 25 blocks to Pennsylvania Hospital's birthing suite.

6:05 a.m.: "Oh, you're Dr. Galbraith's Mom. She's over there."

I enter a Day's Inn type room and try to fold my 5-foot, 9-inch frame into a small package. Staff and surgical paraphernalia surround me. Bright and cheery professionally trained dispositions abound. Their smiling chattiness camouflages immense skill. A nationally reputed birthing center, Pennsylvania Hospital hourly orchestrates easy and excruciatingly difficult deliveries. I feel lucky to be here but decide not to think about potential disasters.

6:15 a.m. "Come On, Sara," I cheer silently. Knowing how interactively intelligent pre-birth beings are, I have been talking and singing to Sara for weeks. Michael stands at the bed, following directions from wife and nurses. "No, hold my hand a little further down." He and I exchange a brief glance that says, no matter how skillful, deliveries contain inherent risk. We both want this birth successfully completed.

6:30 a.m.: "Second babies are a different delivery situation than first babies" the obstetrician sees a quick entry. At ease and in charge, she looks at me, calculates her options, and says, "Mom?" I nod. I feel very lucky to be here.

6:45 a.m.: a shock of wet umber hair is the first evidence of Sara, who slithers into our lives with vehemence. She moves her head jaggedly. Wrinkled but alert, she opens an eye partway, and begins to wriggle. A nurse's pat in the right place, and Sara squeaks briefly, then announces her arrival with a bellow in a voice bigger than this tiny person. The kid is going to be a belter, a squeaker, and a wriggler. Understated elegance of her name aside, the personality I just saw portends that Sara Grace Galbraith is going to impact our world. Just watch.

7:10 a.m.: First bath complete, miniscule pink and blue striped cap covering her temporary post-birth pointy skull, Sara looks exquisitely beatific. Her skin has become robustly pink.

31

Her lips, still puffy from her nine-month aquarium, put ads for lip gloss to shame. Her large eyes, alternately wide open and closed, announce intelligence. She wraps tiny tendrils around the stalk of the long index finger I inherited from my pianist mother. Quietly breathless, I feel …well…reverent.

My experience has been informed by recent research. Well before birth, infants are distinct individuals. They intuit much about our world from their belly aquarium. Dr. Alison Gupnick, reports that babies are born with high intuitive grasp of complex human needs and resources. Newborns believe that people are special and intuit crucial links between their own internal reactions and the internal feelings of others. For example, researchers found that if they stick their tongue out at a newborn, the newborn will mimic the reaction, indicating that newborns can link their own internal kinesthetic sensations to those of another person. This ability enables infants to form the attachment to adults crucial to their welfare. The system is simply brilliant. And Sara has just demonstrated it without any instruction.

Looking forward to future time with my new granddaughter, I decide that I will try this experiment. Next time I see Sara, I will stick out my tongue at her and see if she returns the gesture. Who knows? She just might. So far, child development research has been really helpful in knowing what lurks inside keen minds that cannot yet tell us just how many of our secrets they have precociously deciphered.

To consider: What do you think infants know before they are born? How do you know? Might you like to learn more?

JUST THE FACTS

Brad sounded worried when he talked about leaving the therapist he had worked with in Minnesota. Tall and confident in his career as a human resources manager for a Fortune 500 company, Brad managed to carry himself elegantly despite his constant anxiety, depression and acid reflux. Plagued by ulcers for much of his adult life, Brad had found that talking with his therapist had calmed him down and helped him to think straight. However, after five years of weekly therapy, the anxiety and depression that plagued him continued, and the acid reflux still required ongoing medical attention. Relocating with his wife to the Delaware Valley, she had encouraged him to seek therapy that might help him to master his anxiety and depression. Although Brad liked the idea of structured lessons on how to outthink depression, he was fearful about changing the type of therapy. When Brad and his wife and I met, Brad asked some legitimate questions about how to evaluate therapy.

"I was worried about how long the therapy was taking but

my therapist in Minnesota explained that I needed to understand how my family upbringing impacted my anxiety and depression. He was pleased with the progress we made in the five years. I asked him about the newer approaches that provide research about the effectiveness of the approach, but he said these things are very hard to measure, so I shouldn't worry about the research. That confused me even more. How do I know if therapy was working and what shall I do next?" His steady gaze met my eyes as he asked me to help him figure out what to do next.

Skills based credentials: therapy has often been called the "talking cure," since the exchange of words between the client and therapist looks like what is going on. In reality, therapy offers much richer experience than the simple exchange of words and advice. Psychotherapists have been solidly trained in clinical nursing, psychology and social work. Since anyone can hang a shingle and advertise himself or herself as a psychotherapist, it is crucial to know how to recognize credentials. These include substantial knowledge in their field of expertise, decades of experience in clinical practice, passing exams for certification from professional associations, academic publications in area of expertise, and business skill. Other values include integrity, sound judgment, enthusiasm for their work, and ability to connect with others. The field is intensely skills based.

What is therapy worth? Locally, a Ph.D. with 15 years of training may charge up to $300 hourly for their skills, while a less credentialed clinician may work for the $40 paid by the insurance company for brief managed care work. As in other professional realms, greater training, skill and experience is customarily more costly, and is sometimes valued more highly.

Evaluating therapy: to help Brad evaluate his earlier therapy,

I encouraged him to ask himself these questions and suggested that the answer to each question needed to be a firm, "Yes!"

1.Did you set therapy goals for the first year of your work and did you achieve them within the first year of work?

2.Does your therapist indicate solid and deep expertise in the specific area you need to address? For example, if you seek couples work, what training has your therapist had in this specialty area? Is this indicated through publications, credentials?

3.Does your therapist offer you specific intervention techniques and strategies to address your problems both in the session and at home? Does therapy seep into the corners of your life, your heart, and your values?

4.Do you find that you implicitly trust your therapist's judgment in helping you work out your own answers to your concerns? Is your therapist the catalyst for your growth? Does your therapist "get it" quickly and deeply as you speak with him/her?

5.Does your therapy bring you closer to who you are inside, to the person you want to be with those you love, and to the fullness that your life can bring you? Can you see these changes within the first six months of work?

The Gift of a Life Time: Psychotherapy is a major investment of money, time and energy. It needs to bring you ongoing benefits that enhance your life month after month, or it is not worth your investment. Like Brad, I invite you to ask the questions he asked in evaluating the avenue to personal growth and fulfillment.

To consider: If you are in therapy, is it working for you? If you are considering therapy, how do you find out the credentials and expertise before choosing your therapist? This investment in yourself is worth careful shopping. It could change your life.

WONDER FULL LEARNING

"I sincerely believe that for each child, and for the parent seeking to guide him, it is not half so important to know as to feel. If facts are the seeds that later produce knowledge and wisdom, then the emotions and the impressions of the senses are the fertile soil in which the seeds must grow…Once the emotions have been aroused… then we wish for knowledge about the object of our emotional response. It is more important to pave the way for a child to want to know than to put him on a diet of facts he is not ready to assimilate."
- Rachel Carson, The Sense of Wonder, p. 56

"No, Grammy, Rocky is the little turtle. He is even littler than Gracie." Granddaughter Ava, barely 3, was absolutely certain. Her big cornflower blue eyes looked earnest.

"Bart is the big one, and Spike is pretty big too. I really like Bart. Grammy, do you like Bart too?" Words tumbled. Ava could not stop recounting her evening with the Turtlesinger. Her delight had been instantly engaged at the Avalon Library concert: "Oh, Grammy…it is a turtle! A biiig turtle!" Turtle Toter Charlie did a great job of parading all four turtles right to our noses, up close and personal. To my amazement, Bart and Rocky stared unflinchingly back at me. This was not my expectation of turtle behavior, but I was there to learn, and turtle crooner Karen Buckley held my attention with "Turtlebug."

Ava wanted to know more about turtles: "Grammy, does Bart sleep in his shell?" Three years old is a time when interest can promote intense learning. As Rachel Carson reminds us, the sense of wonder is inspirational. And, I am here to report that the enthusiasm is infectious. Ava's interest sparked me to heretofore unasked questions: Just how does one train a turtle?

This summer Ava seemed equally taken with seashells, blowing bubbles, turtles and flowers. Ava discovered flowers some months ago when she helped me care for our windblown gardens. I taught her to sniff the flowers rather than damage them by plucking the blossoms. On one of our walks next to the manicured gardens near the 96th Street Bridge, I saw Mandeville trained to grow on white twine. Seeing that a healthy pink blossom the size of my palm had dropped from the plant, I retrieved it from the sidewalk for Ava. Carrying her treasure home, Ava and I put it in water, where she talked lovingly to it. "Oh, fwower, do you have enough water? "It withered, but she neither cared nor noticed. Her delight and wonder were larger than the life of that lone blossom.

Before she returned home last week, Ava and I stopped at a

local market and bought daughter Juliette a bunch of ivory gladiolas rimmed in brilliant coral. Juliette and Ava put them in water and enjoyed them till the flowers wilted. But last weekend, on a family visit, Ava surprised us by raising a worry. Sitting at the table for a snack, Ava proclaimed, "Grammy, Momma frew the fwowers in the trash!" Ava shot her mother a look that said, "I'm gonna tell on you." Ava was worried that her Mother had committed a flower-crime. "Grammy we loooove fwowers! They feel sad in the trash!" Clearly, I had become the flower police, and Ava wanted to know if Momma warranted disciplinary action. I had to smile. After all, Ava was echoing my sentiments. I thought of day after day when I would look at nearby gardens and proclaim, "Ava, Grammy sure loves flowers." And, as a result of her delight, Ava is learning to ask questions about how flowers grow. Who knows? Perhaps her enthusiasm will lead her where it led me…to building one garden after another, in the ground and in window boxes, at Rittenhouse Square, on a Maryland farm, on our bay and marshland decks. What one loves, one cultivates.

Delight…wonder…This is the stuff of learning to love to learn. And this is the stuff of great mental health. Look straight ahead at the forceful swaying of our fall marsh grasses. Look down to the windborne ripples of our marshland channels. Look up at the wingspread of our soaring egrets. Would you like to learn more about how this works? I sure would.

To consider: If you had a small child with you, what might you point out to that child as you walk about town? How might the sense of wonder about our environs enrich your love of learning more about the world around us?

POSITIVE
RELATIONSHIPS

MARITAL GUTS

"Out of the blue, Paul reported feeling bouts of calm euphoria, a mystical sense of all's-right-with-his-life-and-the-universe, a bright future in sight. ... I knew well the state of vigorous calm he meant, a frequent visitor throughout my own life. [p. 290]"
- *Diane Ackerman, One Hundred Names for Love: A Stroke, a Marriage, and the Language of Healing*

As a psychologist and author known for helping tortured couples deepen their love, I am easily saturated by books about coupling. But some years ago an erudite book list pointed me to Paul West, a masterful author married to poet and non-fiction author Diane Ackerman. Paul had written a slightly fictionalized tribute to his wife long before Diane recently took her turn to tell her version of their love story. In this most literary of couples, each extols the other's virtues in rhapsodic and lyrical language: the books are literary baklava: sweet and rich word pastry about their "decades-long duet." Paul's book recounts, "We would sit, ...sometimes marveling that we had met and actually gone ahead, advancing from circumspect reconnoiter to a wordless clinch that said it all. "They took active measures to keep love burning, decreeing Sundays "house days "never to be used for any purpose but each other. And Diane recounts receiving daily morning odes of love, "a little hand-scrawled love note awaiting me, a gung-ho welcome to the world again after a nighttime away. . . . A new note appeared almost every day for

41

decades." Like dual piano virtuosos pulling every tone from passive ivory keys, Paul and Diane bid entry into the internal world of successfully married love. Taken as a set, the books are courageous, self disclosing guides to what marriage actually is.

Their luck changed when, in 2003, West suffered a stroke that blighted his understanding and production of the spoken and written word. A jail sentence, this illness devastated his identity, his ability, and his self respect. "Taking words from Paul was like emptying his toy chest, rendering him a deadbeat, switching his identity, severing his umbilical to loved ones and stealing his manna," Diane says. West was left with only one non-word, "Mem." Diane, many years younger, became Paul's caretaker. Aggressively designing treatment to return his speech and writing ability, she force-fed him a knowledgeable, powerful potion of speech and neurological calisthenics which actually did revive bombed neural pathways. Diane describes in a 2009 book, One Hundred Names for Love, so named because "once upon a time, in the Land of Before, Paul had so many pet names for me I was a one-woman zoo." Names blighted from memory, excruciatingly slowly, Diane rehabilitated Paul's capacity to snuggle in bed with her and reinvent new names. As part of his healing, Paul invented 100 fanciful names including "Avatar of Bright April, Mistress of Wonderment, My Little Bucket of Hair." Over a five year span, her 20 hour per week therapy worked. Triumphantly, but wistfully, she summarizes their marriage after Paul's rehabilitation, "This is what we have made of a diminished thing. A bell with a crack in it may not ring as clearly, but it can ring as sweetly."

As I read Paul's, then Diane's book, I understood that declining functioning towards the end of life can actually create a model of love more powerful than the Disney version. Life teaches us to hold tight to one another. Love offers all that is human and good when all else fails.

But what terrifies us about losing partnered loving? As hard as it is to endure the eccentricities of another person, why bother? The answer is unflinchingly clear: to love is the greatest human need. By finding someone we deeply love, we learn what it means to be human. As Paul summarizes,"We got accustomed to each other's oddities and became almost intoxicated with them: love me, love my club foot, my tic, my shimmy. It was as naked as that"

Do yourself a favor. Please consider your good fortune if the crabby, often self-serving partner of your life is in good health. And do consider what you would do if you could no longer take this constant for granted. Having lost my first life's love to cancer at age 49 in 1991, I stumbled on my very own John Wayne, as I am fond of calling him. John Anderson sauntered into my life to stay 'til death do us part. Is it worth all the work required of me to forge life and love with this sometimes cantankerous, bigger than life genius? Indeed.

To consider: Please do read first Paul's book, then Diane's. Ask yourself, "Who brings me the love that lets me know I am human?" And, if you are alone now, how can I change myself to find a soul buddy?

JUDITH COCHÉ, PH.D.

THE HAPPIEST MARRIAGE IN THE WORLD

I am fortunate. I actually get to turn marriages around from miserable to joyous. I get to give children the gift of a future with happy parents. I work with couples determined to rescue, revive, resuscitate, and recapture marriages headed for divorce or terminal loneliness.

When summer comes, I love to create the rich food flavors of Provence, France. Have you ever thought of the parallel between creating fabulous and nourishing meals and cooking up your own fabulous and nourishing marriage? In summer of 2009 I began to jot down parallels: after office hours I often enjoy dining on luscious Mediterranean dinners on our marshlands deck. For Christmas that year, partly tongue in cheek, I drafted a rough edition for The Herald, of "Dr. Coche's Recipe for the Happiest Marriage in the World". Recently I dusted off the recipe and found that it creates a breezy list of gourmet coupling ingredients.

Last month I met with Aric and Jeanine, a clever couple who

had taken our communication skills workshop to freshen up a 45-year marriage. Aric, a retired corporate consultant to the science industry and his wife, Jeanine, followed up the course with a consult. I began by asking how the active listening and negotiating skills were going. Art looked embarrassed. "Not well. It is agony for me to talk about how I feel. And I know I should listen more deeply but it tries my patience."

Janine interrupted harshly. "To be perfectly honest, after all these years of hearing Aric complain, I don't really want to hear how he feels." She looked oddly smug and I wondered what her Cheshire cat grin meant. It seemed out of place.

"Does it make you happy to know that you do not care what your husband thinks?"

"No, but I need to be honest. Everybody thinks we have this great marriage. If they only knew. It can be brutal."

The interchange between them clarified my confusion. "You both are living in that special kind of loneliness reserved for couples who know how to appear intimate to others but who feel doomed to a barren emotional life together. Now I know why you came all the way from New York. You really need to inject fresh energy into your sluggish marriage." They nodded.

To move energy into a positive direction, I began by handing them a copy of my recipe. They smiled as they read it, and I asked Art and Jeanine to rate their marriage in terms of each of the ingredients:

1. Needs tons of improvement
2. Needs improvement
3. OK
4. Not too bad but could use polishing
5. Wow

After you read the recipe below, grab a pencil. Rank your relationship on each ingredient:

The Happiest Marriage in the World

This recipe serves two, but nurtures all children, grandchildren and friends who know the couple.

Baker's Dozen Ingredients for the Happiest Marriage in the World:

1. Commit fully to the self-discipline needed to practice skillful loving each day
2. Insist on habits to maintain financial security
3. Maintain a sense of humor regardless of the severity of any disaster
4. Prioritize forgiveness of yourself and your partner
5. Pleasure one another, creating joy on all levels each week
6. Build a foundation for safe sexual vulnerability through total honesty, especially when it hurts
7. Celebrate your shared history at each holiday and family event
8. Listen fully to your partner, especially when you do not want to hear what is said
9. Honor a private time to be alone with each other each day
10. Appreciate the differences between you and your partner
11. Discipline yourself to treat your partner like your best friend
12. Minimize harshness and maximize hugging, kissing and snuggling each day

13. Walk tall with pride next to your beloved

This recipe requires a lifetime of simmering to blend the flavors to perfection.

The goal is to have your relationship provide you with some of the happiest moments of your life time. And that is a great gift indeed.

To consider: Look at your ratings. How many scores of 5 do you see? How many would you like? How can you break through to the happiest marriage in the world?

JUDITH COCHÉ, PH.D.

HOW HAPPY IS YOUR MARRIAGE?

Decade after decade, I work with the unhappiest of marriages: lonely couples living parallel lives, bitterly attacking each other in public, having clandestine affairs. Last week I was deeply touched as Art, a distinguished businessman with white hair and deep brown eyes, wept quietly. After five years of intense psycho-therapy for each partner and the couple, Jan, his wife of 39 years had announced that she was finally strong enough to leave him unless he made her a top priority in his life. " I will leave you if you keep putting me last. Mark my words because you won't hear them again. You barely come home, then you are gone again to a board meeting. You want it all and no life has it all. Pick your poison: either modify your career or say goodbye to me."

Art blanched, clearly trying to resist her words. But the determination in her face forced him to take her seriously. "Actually, I would give anything to grow old with you. I want to lie next to you each night until I die. I can't believe it has come to this." Tears forming in the corners of his eyes, he reflected, "I would give it all up for a real marriage. You have raised our children while I have been at work. You have made us a beautiful home. You have cared for my mother to let me get to the top of my field. Now it is our time for a happy marriage and I may have ruined my chances."

Jan closed her eyes to block out the pain she saw in the face of the man she loved. "If you mean it, make me a priority before I am not here to care. I love you more than anyone other than our children. I want nothing more than for you to take me in your arms, but you have not done that for 4 years. So I have convinced myself that being single is better than this. At least if I am single I can find a boyfriend."

The most crucial skill for human well-being is knowing how to love. Maslow, the psychologist best known for creating a hierarchy of human needs, ranked the need for belonging and loving as second only to the need for human health and safety. Loving well is essential to human happiness. Most of us are aware of a pulsating, demanding human drive to create the sense of well-being provided by a human partner. There is no adult love equivalent to sexually seeded love between adults, which is so powerful that it has the capacity to both augment and plunder human well-being. The way we love our partners, our children, our parents, our friends and our pets literally predetermines our own sense of physical and emotional well-being.

Here is a little quiz to help you know if your marriage is in trouble. This little quiz to help you see if you are on the road to a deeply troubled marriage, was developed by Drs. Whisman, Snyder and Beach. It is solidly researched so you can take the results seriously. Simply answer the questions below with "True" or "False."

1. I get pretty discouraged about our relationship sometimes.

2. My partner often fails to understand my point of view on things.

3. Whenever I'm feeling sad, my partner makes me feel loved and happy again.

4. My partner and I spend a good deal of time together in different kinds of play and recreation.

5. My partner has too little regard sometimes for my sexual satisfaction.

6. There are some serious difficulties in our relationship.

7. Minor disagreements with my partner often end up in big arguments.

8. Just when I need it the most, my partner makes me feel important.

9. Our daily life is full of interesting things to do together.

10. Our sexual relationship is entirely satisfactory.

To score, give yourself one point for each "True" for # 1, 2, 5, 6, and 7 and one point for each "False" to # 3, 4, 8, 9, and 10.

Warning sign: If you score more than 5 points, your marriage is on a rocky road. Art and his wife each had imperfect scores of 9 items each, a sure sign that professional help was needed.

To consider: What constitutes a happy marriage? How many of us live in happiness? What did we do to get there? It could just change your life. For the better.

SISSY POWER

No matter how hard I tried, I could never manage to add a sister to my life. And try I did: I asked for a sister for my birthday year after year. So did my daughter, but she got lucky. Because I remarried, I managed to snare two wonderful sisters for my daughter in the wedding package, and all three women are delighted. They giggle, talk about me behind my back, and love each other thoroughly. Giving my daughter two older sisters has been one of my greatest gifts to her.

Since the relationship is not one I experience daily, I was surprised when my cousin Claire, herself the younger sister of two daughters, mentioned that she had gotten a wonderful spoonful of wisdom before the second of her two daughters was born. A friend had told her: "You are the most important person to your older daughter. But your older daughter will be the single most important person in your younger daughter's life. Don't ever overlook that."

This statement might have been hard for me to absorb, had I not seen the energy between older granddaughter Ava, nearly five, and tiny, robust sister Sara, not yet two. They call each other "Sissy" in that special language that sisters develop, and they operate with dynamics I usually associate with well -functioning marital couples. Ava not only watches out for Sara at every turn, she has the competitiveness with her younger sister usually reserved for equally qualified applicants for the same executive position: The beautiful dark haired, blue eyed Ava is subtle in her attempts to jostle Sara, with huge hazel eyes peeking from blond bangs in her round face, from her honorary place as "just about the cutest thing on two legs."

Sara walks like a lumber jack in her well-filled leggings and tummy hugging tops. Throwing out her tummy, shoulder back, all 30 inches of her marches independently forward so a saunter with her on Stone Harbor's 96th Street brings constant smiles from well-dressed ladies strolling the shops. In public, Ava is the perfect older sister: polite and protective, she helps "Sissy" reach high items in shops, and reminds me if I forgot to buckle her seat belt. Ava is so lovingly protective that Sara has her own bodyguard. Sara and Ava are so devoted to one another that, on a recent trip I took with Ava, she told me that she missed "Sissy" before she told me that she missed Mommy and Daddy.

However, sisters share complex and layered relationships, and a few hours with Ava and Sara tells the rest of the tale. In private, when the two need to share one beach wagon or one package of cookies, the rivalry pops out. Sara's first words included, not only "Dada," but "MINE!," uttered with all the assertiveness in her tiny body. There is no hitting or yelling: other than the occasional two-year-old outburst, the two work out differences through wining, asking for an adult to judge who plays with the only red wagon, and who gets attention.

As the first grandchild of four child-centered grandparents, Ava has had quite an adjustment. But, for her hard work, Ava reaps adoration and wide-eyed heroine worship: If Ava uses the big jungle gym, so must "Sissy," who pushes to be like Ava by fearlessly taking on heights. If Ava wears a bow in her long silky brown hair, Sara insists on gathering her sandy wisps into a bow-topped arrangement, creating the appearance of a decorated apple. And, if adoration weren't sufficient, Ava is also undergoing leadership training fit for executive tasks: "Sissy, you need to wear a hat in the sun," "Sissy, you need to go for your nap."

Cambridge University scholar Terri Apter interviewed 76 sisters from 37 families and has captured well the complexity of sisters, who customarily combine deep love with rivalry, just as we see with Sara and Ava. Theories of human development report that female relationships often combine a mix of emotions—loyalty and disinterest, love and hate, envy and admiration. Sisters' relationships can be as influential in determining in adult personality as the parental relationship: sisters both need to differentiate themselves from one another and cherish the deep protectiveness they feel for the same person. For this reason, a sister's death can be devastating, and adult female friendships often capture the dynamics formed in early sister relationships.

To consider: Cousin Claire's wisdom is worth contemplating. Do you agree that the most important single influence to a younger sister is her older sister? And how might this awareness impact your life?

"JUST OLD?" A WHITBY TAIL

Whitby Anderson scratched with all his might. Sound asleep, he wriggled onto his back and swatted his head with his black and white paw. The soft graying hair on his teddy bear ears took a beating as he tried to stop the itching in both of his ears. Unable to get relief for the pain, he kept scratching and began banging his head on the floor in his sleep. My heart went out to him, and I bent down and scratched his ears for him. He woke momentarily, thanked me with the huge brown eyes that hold the wisdom of the world, and slipped back into sleep.

The next morning, John and I told Whitby to "Go pee."This daily ritual has been a constant in his life, but on this morning, Whitby looked as though he had no clue that we had addressed him. Worried, we looked at each other and said "Sudden deafness?"Walking to an area where he could not see me, I called again. Whitby simply did not hear. Not only was he in tremendous discomfort, he had suddenly gone deaf. Deeply saddened, I wondered how he would maneuver the city streets and the beaches that are his homes. Would he get killed in traffic? Would he never hear the sound of my voice again? Tears surprised me as I looked at my nearly 12 year old best buddy and mourned the passing of his perfect health.

One vet visit later, we had ear drops for an acute infection in both ears, but little hope. Our vet said "At eleven, he is old. Old age can take hearing. But we can try to improve things." Two weeks of meds later, Whitby was still writhing in pain, still stone deaf…and depressed. The bright-as-a-button guy had gone lethargic. Locked into a world of silence, he could not understand what had happened to him. Although he was trained to follow hand signals through his therapy dog work, and could hear clapping hands, he was not ok. My sadness was profound and the clients who love Whitby daily were very worried.

Ryan Animal Hospital is a world class Veterinary training ground at Penn. I needed to get to the bottom of the diagnosis, so we did a neurological evaluation that diagnosed Whitby with "profound hearing loss in both ears." The neurologist said that nothing could be done because Whitby was "just old."

I discussed this catastrophe with my deaf dog. "Whitby," I said, "You are suddenly "just old. "You are fit and full of life, but you have suddenly been proclaimed damaged goods." Whitby stared plaintively from his silent home.

Feeling plain awful, I asked our vet for ideas. She and I concurred on a second specialist, so Whitby and I consulted Dr. Greg Griffiths, a canine otologist at Penn. Competent and kind, he reported that the auditory canal had narrowed. He suggested steroids followed by an ear flush under sedation. The cost? Just under $1000. Would it help? He thought so but there was no guarantee. Would he do it for his dog? Absolutely! So husband John and I gave the go ahead. It was a no-brainer.

Ear flush completed, Whitby's hearing immediately improved slightly. When we screamed at him, Whitby cocked his head and looked at us…he could hear us. His depression left. Delighted, we trudged back to Dr Griffiths for more improvement, and got it. Whitby is receiving topical steroids. As of today, 40% of his hearing has returned.

John and I have invested over $1000 in treatment for a dog diagnosed as "just old." As a result of our investment, Whitby can hear my voice when I call him loudly. And he wags his tail vehemently when I sing vigorously to him on our daily walks. For his 12th birthday on June 8, he has been given a very big present…. his hearing. Was it worth it? You betcha!

Mental health costs, like veterinary medicine, are too often considered a luxury. We know people who prefer to wait for free care rather than pay for therapy. I feel sad for them. They live with unnecessary ailments that require specialists but they see no wisdom in special care. I want to tell them Whitby's story, but I think that they may not get the point.

Might I invite you to consider that mental health costs are worth every penny? For me, returning partial hearing to our fuzzy faced senior citizen was a brilliant use of my pennies. Life can be much better when you invest in the best for yourself and those you love.

To consider: Might a mental health specialist help me live my life better? If so, would that be worth the investment? Need I feel "just old" or "just depressed" or "just anxious"?

MEANING

A YEAR LIKE NO OTHER

As if it were not enough that, during one week in June, my husband legally died three times, our beloved therapy dog Whitby, passed away from old age that same June week. This combination of catastrophic events made 2012 a year unto itself. Even the year my 48 year old late first husband was diagnosed with, and died from melanoma, did not have the rollercoaster quality of the emotional whirlwind that moved me from despair to jubilance. 2012 has refreshed my deep awareness of the power of the self to know what is right and to do it. People seek meaning at all cost.

Active Wisdom is a time of harvest during second adulthood that allows people to refresh their search for meaning in their lives as they move beyond their first half century of life. In this piece we focus on the search for life meaning that propelled John to his current state of well being.

In June 2012, my seemingly healthy and robust husband slumped at the wheel from a sudden and unpredicted heart attack. We were driving home slowly from a beautiful family beach photo shoot when his heart stopped. Cape Regional Hospital helicoptered him to The Hospital of the University of Pennsylvania, where our adult children and I monitored his bedside in intensive cardiac care for three weeks. Terror gripped our family for about six weeks, while this beloved husband, Dad to six adults and Pop Pop to 4 small children, turned around multiple system damage. John showed us that he intended to return to prior functioning despite all odds. The odds were great against his success so, to rebuild the damaged parts of his body, John needed to rearrange his life priorities.

A man of Mensa intelligence, high moral fiber and extreme skill, John was 50 when I met him. He was running an 8 minute mile and working as a CEO in scientific publishing. But over the next fifteen years, John stopped running and working out in favor of building safe and rich lives for those he loves. On many days, John took better care of our multiple real estate investments than of himself. I learned that warning him of potential danger was of no use. Life had to teach John.

Last June, faced with what I call his "Coming to Buddha moment", John had not one second of doubt: life holds great meaning for him so he decided to focus on excellent self care. "Nothing is more important than exercise," he often states flatly as he maintains his rigorous daily program of cardiac rehab, walking and nutritional discipline. As a result, John has beat the odds. He has just about regained his previously superb level of physical and intellectual functioning and is a more relaxed and self-focused version of the same John I married. He monitors each day, refusing to do too much of what now feels is extraneous to his best interests. At the close of this year unlike any other, the loving and super responsible John Anderson is reminded of what it means to love himself.

I also know others who extend their prime years by daily self discipline. Jack, an old friend, maintains agility in his 80s through swimming and walking regardless of the windblown winter. Diane, a courageous 64 year old client, maintains a superb program of weekly physical therapy, Pilates and walking, which has actually postponed the need for neurosurgery for four years to date. Despite the huge time and energy commitment, John, Jack and Diane take charge of what is within their capacity to change because their lives mean so much. Their courage, tenacity and wisdom is inspirational. Cicero, pegged it when he said that "Diseases of the soul are more dangerous and more numerous than those of the body. " Had my husband John, now healthy and sound in the room next door as I write this, been less focused on winning his battle to regain and maintain his health, he would not be in the room next door.

To consider: What would you do if a health catastrophe happened to you or your family? Do you have the personal resolve to rearrange your life to put your own care first? And who would support you in this effort?

PENELOPE'S WATER WALK

"What matters, therefore, is not the meaning of life in general but rather the specific meaning of a person's life at a given moment."

• *Viktor Frankl*

Next to me, a male voice bellowed from behind a video camera, "Oh baby, you're doing great! Just a little more sweetheart, I promise. Daddy is so proud of you!" Hazel eyes as big as saucers, Penelope looked bewildered as she felt the warm water mysteriously creep past her ankles, higher and higher until she was floating, fully suspended in aquatic space. "Oh, sweetheart, do you like that? Daddy thinks you might like that. You look so, so…peaceful! Just wait 'til our family sees how well you are doing. They will be so happy!"

My take, which I kept to myself as I watched this drama unfold, was that Penelope not only disliked her watery surrounds, but, since she was held by a hand surrounding her small life jacket, knew she was licked and was resigned to her fate. I sat mesmerized as she floated, chin bobbling, unable to fight the rising water than had removed her ability to resist anything. Penelope, an 18-year-old tabby cat with soft grey striped fur, was receiving her first hydrotherapy treatment at Center City's Whole Animal Gym.

Trying to show no surprise in my voice, I asked the man his rationale in selecting water therapy for his cat. (I would have made a different choice, given that every cat I have known hates water.) This sophisticated, well-informed 50'ish man replied, "I have had many cats, but Penelope is really special." His eyes got misty. "She means the world to me. This can help her enjoy her senior years, so it is worth the effort."

Then I understood. Life takes odd detours, creating wise decisions that one never planned. What took me to this situation is that Whitby Anderson, our legendary canine staff member at The Coche Center, has developed back trouble. At 13 plus, or 95 human years, surgery seems unwise, but, to reduce swelling and pain, our vet suggested medication, supplements, acupuncture, and physical therapy. Oddly enough, this seemed reasonable, so Whitby now goes to his very own gym. Unlike Penelope, he likes his time, especially the treats and 30 minutes of pats.

Finished for the day, I wished Penelope well, and, walking Whitby slowly to our car, mused about how deeply our pets infuse our lives with meaning.

At the heart of flourishing is the sense that we are engaged in activities so meaningful to us that we are certain they are worthwhile. When an activity generates well being (even submerging an aged cat in water), high functioning people choose to do the activity for its own sake. Penelope's owner loves this cat and is proud to help her thrive in her rarified 18th year of feline life, just as I offer Whitby his personal work out center. These unusual choices make perfect sense when you understand the way healthy people doggedly (no pun intended) pursue happiness.

At The Coche Center, we assume that healthy humans require meaningful lives. We derive meaning by engaging in something more global than our own life that also is considered important by others. In Whitby's case, our clients are both relieved and admiring when they hear that I have found a non-invasive treatment for his senior aliments. The support of others helps me return to the gym with Whitby, just as the support of his family will help Penelope's owner have the tenacity to submerge her in water to strengthen her hind legs. The opinion of others contributes to what one considers meaningful. But, even without the praise of others, maintaining the health of a beloved four-legged family member provides many of us with a very deep level of life meaning.

Penelope's owner and I are also demonstrating other features of a flourishing life in pursuing treatment for our pets. We show:

1. Optimism by selecting an infrequently chosen treatment. We have been advised by experts that this is likely to help.

2. Resilience by choosing an obscure answer to a problem, even if others judge the choice as foolish.

3. Self determination by researching our choices.

4. Vitality through continued enthusiasm for our decision.

5. Positive relationships by supporting the animal, which has enriched our lives through, continued loving companionship for over a decade.

In the final analysis, pursue what means the most. Pursue with enthusiasm, and watch your life flourish.

You'll be glad you did. To consider: Which unusual life decisions have you pursued? Are you glad ?

THE WOMAN WHO GAVE HERSELF AWAY

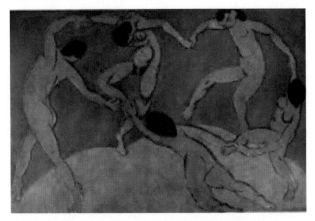

"No, I don't want to be in cold, wet England in February, I get sick there and stay sick till spring. But my daughter tells me I owe it to her to visit while she is abroad, so I guess I'll have to go." Shoulders drooping into her rounded stomach, Jana looked around the room at her women's therapy group members. They knew her very well.

"What would be so bad about saying no?" Lila, intuitive as usual, took the lead. "Why give up on your own health and pleasure to comply to her demands again? You lose your voice in cold rain. We remember that from last time. Stay here."

"If my daughter dared demand that I do something this risky for my health, I would tell her to grow up and be real!" Tall and sparkly, Mary Jeanne had won the group's respect by raising two successful daughters while building a thriving real estate business.

Jana's sigh created a thick fog in the therapy room. "The worst part is, with four adult kids and four grand kids, I am always running behind their requests no matter what I do. "Her small softly rounded frame slumped in the black leather couch in the Philadelphia offices. "I spent my whole life taking care of my husband and these children, and now that he has died, I want nothing at all. I see no future." She looked despondent.

But you are funny, smart, with it, loving, and you have great taste in clothes. Some man would be really lucky to find you. Sorry if I sound annoyed, but I get so impatient when you give yourself away to these kids! They only demand things of you because you let them! They do not need you to complete their lives because you raised them well. Stop giving into their every whim. You have somehow trained them to take advantage of you lately. When will you get it and change?" Callie, a stridently successful single architect, barreled forward. "We have been over this and over this and we can't help until you help yourself. This group cares more about you than you do." She spoke eloquently for the others: as I looked around the room, heads nodded in agreement.

"Jana, the group agrees with Callie and Lila. They are on your team, but are at an impasse to help you as long as you do nothing different. Does that make sense?" I used self discipline to prevent impatience from creeping into my voice, aware that my angry tone could slow down Jana's needed change. "How much do you want to be home in February watching a chick flick with one of your wonderful friends, in front of your stone fireplace?"

Jana began to tear up. "That would be wonderful. Do you think I can do it?" Since I did not actually have the confidence that her core was solid enough to withstand this pressure from her daughter, I remained silent, thinking that by next year she would be able to say no.

"Will you try?" Lila chimed in. "Will you please friggin' try? You deserve this. Do it for your daughter if you can't do it for yourself! It is not good for her to be able to manipulate you and you know it." The silence of Jana's response was deafening in the room. Jana was not yet able to meet her own needs first.

Lack of core identity is often at the root of seemingly superficial problems. Jana is only aware of having demanding adult children, but, on closer examination, the children have been trained to be demanding by a mother with precious little sense of self. Her core personality dysfunction creates the behavioral problem that she attributes to her children. Treatment needs to center around her core personality dysfunction, or lack strength in core identity.

Can we treat core personality issues like poor self esteem successfully in psychotherapy? The good news is that personality transformation is the stock in trade of depth therapists, who combine behavioral management techniques with transformational personality treatment. Individuals who suffer from diagnoses grouped under the rubric, "Personality disorders" can turn to psychotherapists who employ training and patience to transform dysfunctional personalities. Yes, adults crippled by early experiences can reclaim successful lives. Can Jana change? Absolutely. Will she? That is up to her.

The powerful circle of women helping women has created a new chance for Jana. She no longer needs to give herself away. I invite you to look inside yourself to see whether your personality needs a tune up. Do you, like Jana, give yourself away to the loudest bidder? Does your self-sacrificing behavior bother those who love you? Are you so painfully shy that you shrink from the love you need and want? The personal emotional training that individual and group psychotherapy has to offer you actually could brighten your future. And grabbing for that brass ring is up to you.

To Consider: Do I dare tackle my own tendency to limit myself in harmful ways? Would I consider getting the help I know I need? Why or why not?

JUDITH COCHÉ, PH.D.

THE HEART BENEATH THAT HARD SHELL

Love is our true destiny.
We do not find the meaning of life by ourselves alone-
We find it with one another.

• *Thomas Merton*

It is indescribably delicious to watch a love triangle. It heightens the senses, leaving many questions unanswered. It titillates both body and intellect. Earlier this month, granddaughter Ava and I witnessed a remarkable trio working out the complexities of their love lives in front of our very eyes. Ava was enchanted with the story behind their escapades, and she is not yet five years old. When we were invited to the homes of Bart, Gracie and Rocky, we did not know we would be privy to observe this drama. We were drawn into their private sphere as though we were old friends. Perhaps, as a result of our time together, we are.

The demonstration of affection took place on a grassy patch on the marshlands on a beautiful early summer day. Bart, large

68

and masculine in appearance, was ambling slowly around his yard when he spotted Gracie, his petite girlfriend, walking nearby. He slowly bolted towards her tail with unmistakable intentions to hug her by climbing on top of her. Gracie waited patiently, clearly accustomed to the choreography of what was to happen next. Although she is less than half the size of the outgoing and friendly Bart, she was not at all afraid. She welcomed his advances, as though spring had sprung within her and she was ready for love. As gently as he could, Bart climbed her back and rested near her tail. In a few moments, overtaken by the romance of his encounter, Bart began to sing to Gracie. His short pig-like grunts broke the silence of the marshes and pulled me into the unfolding drama. Singing from his heart, his lilting melody was meant only for Gracie. He really only had eyes for her.

But this special moment was not to last very long. Tiny Rocky, less than one quarter the size of Bart, spotted the two and sped in hot pursuit to visit them. Catching the drift of the amorous moment, Rocky got ready to stand his own ground. Not to be outdone by turtles two to four times his size, Rocky attempted to fend off his competition to get to the turtle he found simply terrific. The dynamics were unmistakable: Bart and Rocky were both after Gracie. A bit of research confirmed that turtles are both sociable and amorous. They like to get acquainted with each other by spending time with their possible mate, rubbing against each other to show other signs of affection and making mellow grunting sounds.

I was reminded of the hundreds of marital affairs I have worked with. The difference is simply that Bart, Gracie and Rocky are turtles. Their family, Karen and Charlie, explained that this triangle has existed for a long time, and that Karen and Charlie take care so that nobody gets hurt. Just like human life, turtles love to love each other and are driven to express their love openly.

But what, you may be asking, does the love triangle of three turtles have to do with human mental health? The two are intricately entwined. We are part of a vast assortment of legitimately possible ways to love one another. Just as I love my dog Whitby, Karin and Charlie love their turtle family and are loved in return. And my experience documents that turtles clearly love one another. As Diane Ackerman, naturalist and documentary author suggests, love provides us with an enchanting mystery that runs our lives, regardless of our species. Ackerman observes succinctly, "At some point, one asks, "Toward what end is my life lived? A great freedom comes from being able to answer that question. …From the deserts of Namibia to the razor-backed Himalayas, there are wonderful creatures that have roamed the Earth much longer than we, creatures that not only are worthy of our respect but could teach us about ourselves.""

Listening to Bart croon to Gracie with the timelessness of Bing Crosby, I marveled at how tender we all are under our own variety of the hard shell we wear to protect us. Our defenses create blocks in our ability to love skillfully. Bart and Gracie teach us to love each other so gently that our shells do not get in our way. That visit remains in my memory to remind me how precious life is around and beneath our shells. The hearts protected by those shells require sustenance. It is up to us to provide it.

To Consider: How do you protect yourself from love by hiding under your own hard shell? Is there a better way?

ACCOMPLISHMENT

LITHE LIMBS

We retire too early and we die too young,
our prime of life should be in the 70's
and old age should not come until we are almost 100.
                                                    • *Joseph Pilates*

Catherine Bateson, coined the term "Second Adulthood," to capture ages 55 to 80. This is a time when advances in health allow physical and intellectual flourishing and create time to develop less used parts of the self. We have achieved "Active Wisdom," and are healthy and active. These can be some of the happiest years of our lives. Because Cape May County has many citizens enjoying a second adulthood, there is much interest in how to maximize life after 55. Anna's story tells the tale.

73

At 68, Anna looks to be about 55. Blue eyes grace her narrow, intelligent face and her short blond hair is often wind tousled from working out. She has slowly cut back on a career as an executive coach, and is successfully married to Chad. They enjoy their Ocean City home all summer.

Three years ago Anna began Pilates training, though her private lessons were so costly that Chad wondered if she was "getting her money's worth." Anna is certain that her training prevents typical age-related stiffness and pain. "I am more supple than my friends," she says. She searched for and found a used "Reformer," the Pilates equipment that is similar to a universal gym. Anna often "goes for a ride" in the morning, stretching and strengthening key muscle groups in her legs, arms, and core pelvic area. The learning has been hard: time after time she was tempted to give up, telling herself that she was "too old for this stuff." But Anna said that she keeps plugging because "I feel joyful that I can do this work. My new Pilates expertise keeps my body alive."

Because her dedication was evident to her trainer, she invited Anna into a small class for Pilates instructors. Anna, who still thought of herself as a beginner, was buffaloed at first: the other class participants were less than half her age, and were already Pilates instructors. But, with a bit of encouragement, she took her pride in her hands and tried a few classes. Much to her delight, she could keep up with half the activities. "We do this thing called Short Spine, where you are supposed to rise up on your shoulders with your legs perpendicular to your waist, and then swing your legs down and away from your body till they are flat again on the reformer. It requires more coordination than I have, and it scares me. I was tempted to pack it in, but the trainer took my legs and helped me get into the vertical stance, and then use my pelvic strength to swing my legs gently till they actually landed on the machine. I am still really clumsy but I intend to keep this up till I get it. I am so proud! I am like the little engine that could: I think I can, and, I can!"

I wondered aloud what seemed so crucial to Anna about mastering Pilates. She had led an accomplished life so why start again? Anna had a ready answer: "I am competent in many life areas but had to let my own body work go in order to build my coaching career and I worried that my body would begin to give out on me, like it does so often in the 60s. I actually feel prouder of being able to take this class and work on the Short Spine than I did when my company was named for excellence in 2010. I am using a part of myself that laid dormant for too long. I love this work not only because it feels terrific, but also for the pure thrill of the achievement. To be able to reinvest in my body in my mid 60s has been thrilling. The second wind that Pilates has given me is one of the greatest gifts in the last 20 years of my life. When I coach, I recommend that execs find their passion, pull it out of storage, and that is what this idea of Second Adulthood has been like for me!"

As I heard Anna speak candidly about the thrill in her new found love of taking care of her body, I thought of those I work with, who refuse to do needed self-care, and wished that they could hear Anna's story. And perhaps, through this column, they can.

To consider: Which areas of your life might be lying dormant? Which areas of achievement might enrich your life? How might that be advantageous for you?

NO PERFECT PEOPLE ALLOWED

As I drive weekly between the Philadelphia and Stone Harbor offices, I pass a road sign at the edge of a driveway that makes me smile. In commanding black letters, it heralds "No PERFECT PEOPLE allowed." Driving by the sign, I often reflect on how many clients drive for perfection. Rebecca was one of these clients until recently.

Rebecca's cow brown eyes looked upwards, signaling deep thought. "But my goal is to be a really perfect person." Rebecca meant it. She had spent the last five years careening between disappointments while she lost and gained the same twenty pounds twice. Her choice of boyfriends was so dangerous that she frequently woke with a start, hoping valiantly that one would call her for a midnight tryst that very night. Rebecca found The Coché Center after she took a job that brought her to Philadelphia, where she knew practically nobody. She hated the job and bemoaned her life.

Rebecca was working in cognitive psychotherapy with Stephen Schueller, a trainee at The Coché Center completing his degree in Clinical Psychology at the University of Pennsylvania, where I teach. Rebecca respected Stephen: tall and gentle, he had a searching way of asking questions. "Why be a perfect person? How many really perfect people do you know?"

The question dislodged Rebecca's complacency. "Well…I know zero perfect people."

"Me too," Stephen said, "So between us, we don't know anybody perfect. Right?" Unwilling to consider his implication, Rebecca was quick to retort, "But I want to be happy. Is that too much to ask? Wouldn't I be happier if I were perfect? I think I need to be perfect to be happy."

Stephen continued quietly: "Have you ever considered that continuing to strive for perfection actually keeps you from being happy? Let me help you understand why being perfect and being happy don't go together. You have decided that you need to achieve unachievable future goals in order to happy. You want the perfect boyfriend, a high-paying job, a size 10 wardrobe, and you have none of these. But the good news is that these are not the things that will make you happy. Did you ever consider that humans are imperfect by definition? Perfection is an ideal, but what you want to shoot for is the optimal achievement of realistic life goals. Aiming realistically allows you to feel satisfied with most of your life most of the time." Rebecca nodded, soaking in the wisdom that Stephen offered her.

To feel happy, Rebecca needs to live in the present instead of the future. She needs to be appreciative for the small daily joys of her life, to collect small and repeated moments of enjoyment each day. For her this might mean a satisfying 15 mile bike tour, a cup of green tea with a new girlfriend, a hot shower with fresh lemon bath gel. The drive for perfection actually distracts from enjoying what makes us happy. Instead of perfection, Rebecca might strive to be good enough, enough of the time.

As Rebecca sponged up what Stephen said, her eyes began to dance: "You mean that all these years I've gotten it all wrong and tried to be perfect when I don't have to be perfect at all?"

"Yes. Your goal might be to flourish rather than achieve perfection." Rebecca nodded in understanding, absorbing the new idea with relish. Rebecca has begun her journey. We wish her well.

Dr. Dan Gilbert, a social psychologist, says that if we need to experiment with bits of new behavior aimed at happier lives. We literally stumble towards better answers for our lives. Far from a beeline towards perfection, the growth process is one of experimental investigation. Perfection is merely an idea in our head. Experimentation allows us to shape our attempts until we can make life work better, and making life work makes us happy.

To consider: How might your life change if you abandoned any goal of perfection and replaced it with an emphasis on enjoying more daily moments in your life? What makes you happy each day? What makes you smile inside? Just for fun, try replacing the drive for perfection with stumbling towards people and activities that make you happy. Others just might experience you as more relaxed and fun to be with. And that has to be good.

MY NECESSITY IS YOUR LUXURY

Lucky Lauren found a great self-made guy. The son of a construction worker who built a small contractor business, Matthew got a scholarship to business school and is busy conserving pennies to build his own business dream. Lauren dreams about her wedding bed: $500 taupe king sheets rest under a cloud of pure English down. After hours on the Internet she seized both the "sale" on the web, and the sheets, used Matthew's credit card because her own card had reached its limit, and bought the sheets. When Mathew saw the $500 purchase, he simply lost it: "You bought what?"

Lauren is "hooked" on shopping. She knows Matthew considers her addictive spending a deal breaker. Lauren has no way to think about how to spend. Aware that the post-divorce weekends with Dad substituted solo shopping for time with Dad, Lauren knows that Life Style has long been synonymous with love. We began to address the concern. Relieved at the homework assignment we devised, Lauren spent her shopping hours learning to use an excel-based budget and actually enjoys recording purchases in clothing, nails, food, travel.

The couple needs help in defining the meaning of money in building a life together. Matthew envisions years of emotional bloodshed trying to support a life he cannot afford. The couple lacks respect for the taste and spending of the other, and they are headed for trouble. I began to describe that one person's necessity can be another person's luxury and that both positions can be legitimate. They perked up. This was something new. What did I mean?

I explained that our values drive our spending. How we think determines what we buy. I described three levels of expenditures. We talked about necessities, investments and luxuries, and how one person's luxury is actually another person's necessity. We agreed that each of us has a spiraling set of needs that define who we are, and that financial security rests on being able to afford one's purchases. We chose typical items and asked each partner to decide whether this was a necessity, an investment or a luxury in a particular life situation.

A necessity allows satisfaction of basic thirst, hunger, sexual desire, security, career advancement, pleasure. An investment increases the probability that future life goals will be reached if money is invested in the future. It says, "If I spend this money now, I will have better outcomes later." Examples include designer clothing that projects the successful image needed for professional practice development; health club membership to increase fitness and attractiveness. Luxuries are the toys of living. They may bring emotional satisfaction but often run counter to basic security and long-range planning for overall financial freedom.

Lauren and Matthew loved discussing the items we selected. Their job was to decide whether each item was a luxury, an investment or a necessity for them. In so doing, they began to construct their own value system as a couple. Sheets returned, the wedding plans continue.

To Do: Write next to each item below whether you see it as a necessity (N), an investment, (I) or a luxury (l). Do this alone or with a family member.

- Gourmet coffee beans by the pound
- A $45 Haircut of an up and coming executive
- A computer for a bright 4-year-old
- Fresh tuna steaks
- Diamonds to celebrate a 25th anniversary
- Larger house for family with three kids, with fireplace and a family room

Consider your answers. What do they tell you about your values? Why do certain items mean so much to you? How much interpersonal agony might you prevent if you can purchase more simply and modestly?

JUDITH COCHÉ, PH.D.

THEY LIVE IN MY HEART

Sad eyes looking straight at me, Diane paused, gathering strength to say what felt almost unsayable. "My brother got horribly drunk again last night and crashed his car into a tree. He fractured his pelvis and there is nobody to care of him. Of course he does not have insurance. I can't handle him and the two kids with nobody else at home to help me. As I was driving to the hospital last night, worrying that he would die from the injuries, I thought about how helpful all of you are to me. I kept you in my heart while I waited for the medical report. At first I thought he might be paralyzed, and I kept thinking about what you would say to help me stay strong. Between his alcoholism and little kids, it really feels like he is my third kid. I was so scared I could not be angry 'til I knew he would survive the damages, but now I am angry on top of being scared and sad."

Responsive as always, Diane's group was ready and able to help her. Eric, a prize winning advertising executive from a highly disturbed Midwestern family, was the first to speak. "That reminds me of the time I had to talk my Mother out of putting a plastic bag over her head. I was in New York and she was in Kentucky, and there was nobody nearby that she would listen to. It was horrible for me: I could picture hearing that she was dead so I wanted to get on a plane, but I couldn't. You guys were the support team that was with me in my living room that night. I could imagine what each of you would say. Your voices and my stubbornness saved her life. Without you I would have been jelly-bellied and might be living with the guilt of her dying on me."

Amanda jumped in to help Diane. The two had been in group therapy together for three years. They decided that they felt like a Mother Daughter team: At 62, Amanda delighted in Diane's spunky take on raising kids solo, as Amanda had done for decades. "Man, couldn't he at least have stayed sober? I mean, did'ja have to drop your kids at the neighbors at 3 AM and rush to the hospital? You deserve tons of credit for this, Diane. You are so strong! First you raise your kids alone, which I find inspirational, and now you babysit this alcoholic brother all night. That is really impressive."

Graham, a quiet accountant in the group, spoke carefully. "I admire your tenacity. You show that quality of resilience that Judith talks about. How did you stay so strong?"

Diane smiled. "I just kept pushing forward because there was nothing else to do. It is who I am. But knowing that I would report this to my group made that frightening night bearable. I had you all with me waiting for the news from the docs. Three years ago, when I had the good sense to accept Judith's invitation to join this group, I did myself a favor by creating connections to people that care about me and are as smart as I am. You live in my heart between meetings, helping me to make the best decisions for myself."

I smiled. Diane "got it." She understood the power of relationships to increase courage to do the right thing in humanly impossible situations. Therapy group members offer support in and between meetings because they carry each other in their hearts, relying on these internalized relationships to steer them when their lives create struggles of large proportions. I decided to acknowledge the moment. "I want to thank you all for helping Diane by cheering her on while we all slept. This group creates powerful relationships for each of you. You are very fortunate to have each other."

Resilience is the drive that keeps people going in good directions when life sends tragedies and challenges. People who are resilient are by nature relationship-centered. They reach out to others, wanting to help them and receive help in return. In this way they form and maintain fulfilling connections to other people. Diane has formed deeply moving relationships with Eric and Amanda, carrying their voices with her. Forming ongoing relationships of substance creates support for tough times. And that is what resilience is about.

To consider: Whom do I carry in my heart with me to support me when I need that extra help? Have I told them lately how much this means to me?

EPILOGUE

EPILOGUE

When I first started doing psychotherapy in 1978, I naively assumed that success was a word that began with a capital letter "S" for sophistication. As I came to hear the tender stories of people working diligently to transform unhappy parts of their lives, I internalized that success relies on core values stated very simply.

I also revisited my Senior Advanced high school English course and found that one assignment had provided me with great wisdom. Just before graduation, we were required to write a 500 word personal essay about how we planned to live our lives. I had already begun reading Martin Buber, Viktor Frankl and Erich Fromm, so I sprinkled my thoughts with their writings. But I relied mainly on the words of my Father, whose innate wisdom rivaled theirs. Over four decades later I stumbled upon the blue-lined 3 ring binder paper, now brown with age. I read it with curiosity, expecting to be amused by my adolescent ramblings. Instead I found an early statement of my core values. These values would go on to carry me through the premature death of a husband, a remarriage, and a longstanding career in academic and applied clinical psychology. I wrote of planning a life of substance in which loving was my foundation, and of seeking and finding meaning in my life.

Recently I compared what I wrote with current advances in the positive psychology categories that enable a sense of permanent well-being. It became clear to me that Buber, Fromm and Frankl were good choices for my early readings. At 17, with no formal exposure to psychology, I had wished for a life filled with lifelong love, high creativity, lots of fun, and, first and foremost, a sense of meaning. These are the key concepts in the categories that create lives that flourish.

As you look ahead to the future that you are creating, which qualities are central for you in living your best life? Do you have the courage and self-discipline to create a life that allows you to thrive? I hope so.

I wish for you your best life, savored daily with those you love.

UNIQUELY YOU

"Do you really think my work matters to clients? I am never sure. I am only 28 and have so little experience doing psychotherapy with clients." Yoshi's long dark hair framed her serious face. "I wonder if I should just stay in teaching and research where I know I am trained to do the work."

Yoshi had come to the U.S. on a scholarship to get a PhD in Clinical Psychology and, despite inadequate self-esteem, had much to offer. Reticent about speaking up, she had been raised in Japan where she was taught to respect her elders, remain modest, and follow orders. She was less assertive than the self-promoting graduate students in her competitive program and was less applauded by the faculty.

As a clinical professor I have mentored residents and graduate students since 1990. Yoshi was the least confident student I had been asked to mentor. She needed to trust her own abilities to be able to use them to her best advantage.

Yoshi's story illustrates the need for self-esteem. Unlike a plumber, the tool kit of a clinical psychologist is within the clinical trainee, who receives learning in psychological assessment, research, theory, and therapeutic interventions.

Yoshi's insecurity was holding her back. Her voice was so hesitant that clients mistrusted her ideas and professors criticized her work. I was asked to help her "know who she is so that she can perform to capacity in clinical psychology." My job was complex. How much could I do in the 10 months of weekly supervision to help her make needed improvements?

In addition to the more customary readings and meetings, I introduced her to the work of Virginia Satir, a founder of family therapy and champion of the human spirit. Satir had been instrumental in my own training and I have recommended her books to many. I gave Yoshi "My Declaration of Self-esteem" and instructed her to read it often. Short and easy to understand, Satir's writing teaches that the foundation of being a person is the unique combination of talents and love that each of us has to contribute to ourselves and to each other.

"My Declaration of Self-esteem"

- In all the world, there is no one else exactly like me -
- Everything that comes out of me is authentically mine, because I alone choose it - I own everything about me - my body, my feelings, my mouth, my voice, all my actions,
- Whether they be to others or to myself - I own my fantasies, my dreams, my hopes, my fears -
- I own all my triumphs and successes, all my failures and mistakes. Because I own all of me, I can become intimately aquainted with me - by so doing I can love me and be friendly with me in all my parts -

- I know there are aspects about myself that puzzle me, and other aspects that I do not know -
- But as long as I am friendly and loving to myself,
- I can courageously and hopefully look for solutions to the puzzles and for ways to find out more about me -
- However I look and sound, whatever I say and do, and whatever I think and feel at a given moment in time is authentically me - If later some parts of how I looked, sounded, thought and felt turned out to be unfitting, I can discard that which I feel is unfitting, keep the rest, and invent something new for that which I discarded -
- I can see, hear, feel, think, say, and do. I have the tools to survive, to be close to others, to be productive,
- and to make sense and order out of the world of people and things outside of me - I own me, and therefore I can engineer me - I am me and
- I AM OKAY

As you sit on the beach or finish a school year this year, stop to consider your uniqueness in the world. Take a moment to modestly celebrate who you are inside, and think about how your spirit contributes to the lives of those you love. Notice how much you contribute to our world. In the final analysis, above all else, you are what matters most in your life

CLIENTS DESCRIBE THEIR GROWTH AT THE COCHE CENTER, LLC 1978-2013

"One door closes, another opens." A man, 1990

"If you can feel safe in unpredictability, you are alive." A man, 1989

"I've got to get out of the way of myself in order to make myself feel better." A woman, 1992

"I wouldn't be in such a hurry if I knew where I was going." A man, 1990

"I've never had passion with sanity before." A woman, 1988

"I used to think that what I had was a brick wall, but now I think that it is a gate waiting to be opened." A man, 1986

"Boy if this is life, I'll stick around." A previously suicidal man, 1990

"The unknown is always the unknown until you've been there." An 82 year old man finishing therapy, 1987

"I love this group. It's like running with a group of guardian angels." A group member, 1996

"I began to realize that I was alone and the person who helped me most was me." A woman ending therapy, 1989

WELL WISHES:
THE COCHE CENTER, LLC

Our Ph.D. students in Clinical Psychology have benefited from wonderful training opportunities with Dr. Coche for over a decade. The Coche Center encourages young clinicians to stretch themselves professionally to become their best professional selves.
> • Melissa G. Hunt, Ph.D., ACT - Associate Director of Clinical Training, Department of Psychology, University of Pennsylvania

The Coche Center's gifted handling of a variety of clinical challenges has provided state of the art service for clients for 35 years. Dr. Coche's skill in clinical expertise and training is rare.
> • Julian Slowinski, Psy. D., ABPP Department of Psychiatry, Perelman School of Medicine, University of Pennsylvania

I have been working on Dr. Coche's column for five or six years now. It never ceases to amaze me how it inspires, guides, and teaches readers, how to improve their relationships. Her recipe for a happy and successful marriage is both light hearted and packed full of common sense!
> • Joan Nash, copy editor, Cape May County Herald

I enjoy the entertaining columns in the Cape may County Herald. Dr. Coche relates stories with clarity, insight and honesty, making complicated issues more approachable in such a caring way.
> • John A. Tucker, M.D. Dept. of Otorhinolaryngology, Perelman School of Medicine at the University of Pennsylvania

ACKNOWLEDGEMENTS

Deepest appreciation to those central in creating this book:

Paki Tandon, M.A, Taws, and Sarah Hubartt, for best help in putting this little book together

Kudos and appreciation to Martin Seligman, Ph.D., for developing the PERMA categories and educating the public about positive psychology.

To Arthur Hall, publisher, Joan Nash and Al Campbell, editors at The Cape May County Herald, my admiration for supporting mental health education for an interested public.

To the one, the only, John Edward Anderson ,retired publishing executive at The National Library of Medicine and at Biosis, my admiration and love for the capacity to line edit each of my columns, and for providing me very broad shoulders to lean on, no matter when, no matter what.

PHOTO CREDITS

Cover Photo: Jeannie Weber, Avalon Art Photography, photo of Sara Grace Galbraith

A Year Like No Other: Jeannie Weber, Avalon Art Photography. Photo of John Anderson and Judith Coche, Ph.D.

Mobius Image, logo of The Coche Center, Wendy Verna, Octo Design Group

Photos by Judith Coche, Ph.D.:

- I intend to Enjoy It, Photo of Erich Henry Enrst Coche, Ph.D.
- Sailor's Timeless Wisdom, Photo of Whtiby Anderson and Sailor, Portuguese Water Dogs
- How Can You Create Happiness? Photo of Ava lynn Galbraith
- Birth Row, Front and Center, Photo of John Edward Anderson and Sara Grace Galbraith
- Wonder Full Learning, photo of Ava Lynn Galbraith
- Sissy Power, Photo of Sara Grace and Ava Lynn Galbraith
- Just Old, Photo of Whitby Anderson, Portuguese Water Dog
- They Live In My Heart, Photo of anonymous therapy group at The Coche Center

All other photos have free public use

Made in the USA
Middletown, DE
20 February 2020